GOAL SETTING FOR SUCCESS

GOAL SETTING FOR SUCCESS

Turning Dreams into Reality

ROWAN EVERHART

QuantumQuill Press

CONTENTS

CHAPTER 1

Introduction

Throughout the years, we have brainstormed the why and the how about what to do when we didn't know what to do. Each and every time, there was one answer! Setting your goals is one of the best answers to this question and also one of the best strategies that you can use in order to get anything you want. Myself, someone who doesn't speak a word of English and doesn't know the alphabet, ended up learning English and moved on to the US from Turkey. I couldn't achieve this if I didn't know how to set goals and go after how I am going to reach this. No matter what the obstacle is, if you know your destination, point B, sooner or later you will develop the plan to reach that point without knowing how to overcome the obstacles.

It is difficult to accomplish anything without clearly defined goals, and without knowledge of how you can reach this. It is a known fact that if one is faced with a question of "what do you really want in life?" 97% of the people couldn't answer it. Another fact is that 3% of these people are much more successful than everybody else. Goal setting and accomplishment is an art of achieving from where you are to where you want to be. By having a desired goal and a road map of how to get there, you can overcome any obstacles such as depression, grief, anger, or resentment, and you can move on into your future successfully. In this article, we will discuss how to get what you want and go where you want to go.

1.1. Importance of Goal Setting

Meanwhile, some people discourage setting goals. Some of them may not know better, while others claim that goals will stifle creativity, motivation, and enjoyment. Setting challenging but achievable goals does not deaden creativity, reduce enthusiasm, or diminish the joy of accomplishment. Effective and challenging goal setting, in fact, stimulates all of these qualities. It has a profound effect on our mind, our psyche, as well as on how we feel and act. Challenges, even halfway-completed ones, are fun and exciting. They help us stay focused, increase our productivity, and boost our ability to succeed. Goal setting is the single most important behavior that promotes success and achievement. Goal setting truly produces success, influence, or the power to get things done. In summary, your dreams become the specific targets for your goals, or roadmaps, which will help you stay the course and reach your destination. Goal setting will transform what we have into what we want. Goal setting is what takes us from where we are into a better future.

Ralph Waldo Emerson once said, "If one advances confidently in the direction of his dreams, and endeavors to live the life that he has imagined, he will meet with success unexpected in common hours." To advance confidently in the direction of your dreams, you must be able to transform them into concrete and realistic goals that have specific deadlines. These goals are your roadmaps. They take you from dreamland into real life, from a place of wishful thinking to actual accomplishment. While your dreams say, "Wouldn't it be nice if," your written-out goals will say, "This is what I will accomplish by that date, and this is how I am going to achieve it." Goal setting will truly turn your dreams into reality. Goals are the roadmaps to success. Along the way, however, are many smaller goals that you must set in order to eventually achieve the big ones. These smaller steps are necessary to lead you toward overall success and greater fulfillment.

CHAPTER 2

Understanding Goals

Goals are things you do, not things you have so you need to concentrate on the effort and not the outcome. At the end of the day you need to live with the choices you make. Goal setting will help you to realize what you want and will set you on a course for your dreams to come true. The main reason for goal-setting is to help you change the direction of your life. Success is within reach, you merely need to set long-term goals. Goals must be attainable. Goals ignored or not written down become dreams that are short-lived. A goal involves change. A dream does not. Goals lead to what you are and will be tomorrow. Only you have the power to pursue your goals leading to successes within your turn.

A goal is a dream or an ambition with a clearly defined target. The clearer the target, the better the chance of realizing your dream. It's your life so you owe it to yourself to do your best. You're lucky because you have your entire life ahead of you. Renew your six-day energy to set the goal which will lead to what you really want. Have the target within your sight and remind yourself to encourage yourself day by day, especially during the hard and difficult times. The more you talk to yourself, the better you will be.

2.1. Types of Goals

Researchers believe that there are several types of goals, and that different types of goals are important for different reasons. Thus, it is important to note that short-term goals are a distinct and different goal type than long-term goals. While long-term goals may be quantitative in nature, short-term goals may be more qualitative. The SMART acronym states that a goal may be achievable, relevant, and time-bound. One way to make a goal achievable is to begin by envisioning what it would take to meet that goal in a particular time frame. Any action taken can be listed, and combined with consideration of the resources and incentives necessary to ensure a successful completion of work related to these objectives. Information related to a goal may be combined into a plan of action that involves multiple people, whether to provide guidance or to ensure that the individuals who are working for policy and decision makers are following through with the stated goals. If a goal is not achievable, factors that result in success can be identified and put in place.

The acronym SMART has been used to describe the characteristics that are important for goal setting, and due to its widespread use, will be used in this article to support the validity of these insights. The acronym stands for Specific, Measurable, Achievable, Relevant, and Time-Bound. One way to establish a clear target is to turn a vague dream into something that can be represented in non-emotional terms. To this end, it is necessary to state the specific goals to which you are committed and by which you will measure your behavior. When a goal is both specific and measurable, it is also possible to determine when this goal has been met. If a goal is not met in a specific time frame, the goal can be respecified in new, behaviorally measurable terms, or tackled with a different approach.

2.2. Setting SMART Goals

Taking every precaution and using tricks of the trade is essential for traveling with confidence the path that leads us to achieve the objectives: which methods to use, which systems to tackle, how to give structure to the individual strategies, how to focus the energies between the right thing to do and the most urgent thing to do, how to evaluate the results obtained over time, how to distribute the actions to give an organization to activities scheduled over a period of time, how to activate the management system that allows to plan the steps to be followed to complete a complex project. In fact, the real problem is not in finding a system that works. Theoretical models are a dime a dozen, and literature is teeming with them. There are suggestions available for all tastes and for all cases. It means that the effort of the manager or an individual entrepreneur is much more focused on choosing the right method that transforms the objectives into reality. The clear and structured objectives, studied carefully and considered objectively, from each point of view, are halfway. A second preventive optimization is in the choice of the right action plans, in the solutions adopted and in the actions put in place to complete those objectives.

Defining the goals is similar to the action steps taken on a journey, and the clearer they are, the less likely they are to fall into temptation and become transient. In fact, to be effective as a method, they must be concrete, specific and the basic rule from which to depart to shape all the others is that they must present some prerequisites. To be easily identifiable: here is the purpose for which a series of actions are joined together ad hoc. Be easy to understand, without the need for clarification: the same individuals who are called to implement those actions will be able to understand them. Be focused and directly reflect the purpose they are to pursue, leaving out anything that has no functional implications for its implementation.

CHAPTER 3

Creating a Vision

Understanding what is most important to these people is a key to effective and enjoyable goal setting and satisfying and deeply meaningful daily experience. Those in the Zone are living out their individual unique purpose, considering their unique passions, and showing genuine commitment in all areas of life. They constantly feel the inside change of intentional conduct and the outside change of genuine question on this plane. They are inspired and this inspiration shows.

Those living in the Zone, when coming into the present moment, usually comprehend life in big picture terms. Ask them to describe their vision, or how things will look when they have created their lives to the fullest, and they quickly and often eloquently give you a detailed, emotionally connected description of exactly what they want. Those who aren't living in the Zone, who are merely paying the price of doing what they "should" to keep the battle of existence on an even keel, respond clearly, "Hell, I don't know," or "I've never thought about it," or they provide a short and uninspiring answer. That they have a vision is a sign that their particular spirit is taking bat on the playing fields of life and maximizing their life's potential.

This particular spirit is living life the way it was designed to be lived. Not by playing small but expecting and striving to create the big in front of them. Most important, in each of these cases they know why they are taking one step or a great number of steps to get to where they want to be.

The ultimate key to success is to start out by creating a clear and detailed vision of where it is we want to end up. Visions may be inspiring or boring. Goals, once created, may be motivating or uninspiring. Visions and short/long-term goals must inspire action and ignite the flame that keeps the fire of commitment blazing. Indeed, the "why?" must beckon in that direction. In other words, we must attach deep intention to our action.

3.1. Visualizing Success

Mental imagery also fires neurons in the same brain regions that are activated when actually engaging in the experience. These neurons then intensify the physical firing pattern that they represent. The better you can simulate the actual event in your mind, the better your brain will be prepared when it comes time to do it. Scenes may become so familiar it is as if you have already performed them and you develop strong expectations for success. This translates into high levels of confidence. While there is still a need to practice skills directly, a number of studies suggest that mental practice may improve your performance up to 45 percent, sometimes even better than what results from physical practice alone. Another boon of mental rehearsal is that by developing your ability to focus, it may also improve your actual execution of the movements when it comes to doing them for real. Tennis pros have been found to produce more subtle wrist and forearm movements when mentally simulating serves and forehand and backhand shots.

In sports (and in life), visualization is the key way to create any future event. What you see is typically what you get. The more compellingly and frequently you visualize an event – snaring a big client or a promotion at work – the less frequently you will have to engage in the direct practice event to achieve success. For example, psychology students randomly assigned to merely practice five finger exercises on the piano or to practice them in their imagination, were able to learn the notes to a song better than no-practice control students. Moreover, those who played the exercises in their head scored the best. The more realistic the imagery, the better the outcome is likely to be. To make mental practice as close as possible to the actual activity, engage all your senses. For examples, think about how the dirt smells in the baseball game; how the ball sounds when it hits the bat; and how the sun feels on your skin.

3.2. Defining Your Purpose

- If money wasn't an issue and you had unlimited resources, how would you spend your life? - How could you be of service to others, with the intention to help all people be happy and free from suffering? - What would you do if you could not fail? What would make your heart sing in joy? - What is your legacy? - What gives you a real sense of achievement dated at present and in the past? - What do people congratulate you on? - What does the world need that your talents can provide and fix? - What roles do you play in the lives of others, participants and team members and create a culture of antennae, facilitating synchronistic experiences?

Many people have not defined their life's purpose. They live on auto-pilot and have reactions to situations. Defining a life's purpose will help attract the right opportunities and facilitate turning dreams into reality. The following list, by way of example only, provides some preliminary questions to help find your purpose. The expectation is to ask yourself many more questions and choose revealing ones that are right for you. Do not edit or correct yourself; let the answers flow from the heart in free writing exercises.

CHAPTER 4

Developing an Action Plan

Short-term goals are ideal for teens because they have a short attention span and they're really not worried about anything that's going to happen in five years. A large component of long-term goals is working toward something on a daily basis. It's too much to ask a teen to put their faith in something that's not going to happen until they're 20 years old or beyond. More than likely, they're going to lose interest or they're going to tire of the situation because they're not seeing progress. Plan some short-term goals that they can look forward to. The following guidelines provide a structure for helping students break their long-term goals into short-term goals. Remember, these guidelines should be issued on an individual basis, as they are goal-oriented and individualized.

Effective goal planning involves setting short- and long-term goals. A long-term goal is a goal that you plan to achieve over a long period of time, something like in the next five years. A short-term goal is a goal that you want to accomplish soon. Without short-term goals, long-term plans are hard to follow. Short-term goals will lead you towards your long-term goals, helping you lay the foundation for them and building your confidence at the same time. Breaking larger goals into shorter goals is an effective way to cope.

4.1. Breaking Down Goals

Therefore, we thought for some time the things that could be accomplished in future and wrote our goals. The list of our goals was: To be a good entrepreneur; Less dependent on family source income; Good status in our society; Helping others in a good way; To be a role model for our next generations; Free from all debts; Our good old age; Own house; Financial security; Business development. Then we had a question in our mind, how to achieve these goals? How long would it take to achieve these goals? Are these goals SMART? Are these goals realistic? Can we insert meticulous plans or monthly targets and take control of these goals? We had all these questions in our mind and then we asked the trainer. He gave us the answers for all our questions and suggested us to write our vision and mission statements. So, these goals are to be inserted in our vision statement.

At some point in time when the thoughts of entrepreneurship crossed your mind, you wanted to achieve this great dream and thought why not! You have seen so many successful people who have become a role model for all single human beings and you felt that they are no different from you and you have an equal potential and you would like to achieve the heights of success. By speaking to few people or analysing their experiences, you noticed that becoming an entrepreneur would be something which could make your dream come true. But now, you do not know how to start and from where to start. This is what our situation 2 years ago. During this time, we attended a seminar by Dr. Emilio M. Jacinto on Vision 2020. It was a 2 day programme and during the second day in the first session, he spoke about goal setting, targets, aims, we felt like we understood that we got a solution for our problem. We strongly believed that writing our goals could help us achieve our dreams.

4.2. Establishing Milestones

For example, a new author who has just completed and published a book may have as a long-term goal that of becoming a best-selling author who is able to support herself financially from her writing. That is a good goal, but it is not the goal she should first be thinking about. That is a long-term goal. It is often beyond our control and cannot solely be our focus. Milestones are smaller steps that can be accomplished in a fairly brief period of time by taking productive actions. Examples of some milestones for the new author could be: "(1) start being invited for speaking engagements within one year of publication, (2) sell out and reorder at least once within one month of first order, (3) begin working on next book within 6 months of going to press or inside printing deadline." By focusing on these long-term and short-term goals, he or she can more easily achieve success.

Smart goal setting involves establishing milestones, as well as long-term and short-term goals. Milestones are important because they help keep goals in perspective. Some milestones can be achieved more quickly than others. Milestones mark the steps along the way that lead to the final goal. People often make the mistake of setting only long-term goals. Because long-term goals typically will take a long time to achieve, milestones provide the short-term focus that helps keep long-term goals in sight.

4.3. Time Management Techniques

Although time management is important to the goal-setting process, it requires a personal commitment to four basic concepts. The first is assertiveness. Being assertive to your decision-making process allows you the freedom to act and not simply react in each situation.

Secondly, it is important to add organizing your planning skills. By getting organized you will have a place for everything, and then finally putting everything in its place will help you be better prepared for tomorrow, as well as reduce stress and avoid the negative impact of clutter. There are many consequences of poor time management from being disorganized such as failure to meet deadlines, being caught off guard, loss of opportunities, and failed business ventures. The correlation between successful goal setting and time management is that effective time management skills prioritize activities, helps time work for you, and ultimately makes success simpler.

Time management is the process of arranging, organizing, and planning the amount of time spent on specific activities in order to increase effectiveness, efficiency, and productivity. Although successful people come from a variety of backgrounds, the one thing they are all likely to share is effective time management. Among its many benefits, time management increases your productivity and efficiency, helps you maintain focus, and is essential to reducing your stress level on the job and off. We all have the same amount of time in the day, so why do some of us do so much more? It is not the amount of time we have, but how we use it. Time is the one variable that you have complete control over, and what you do with your time is critical to achieving all your goals in life.

CHAPTER 5

Overcoming Obstacles

While we often anticipate various obstacles which may be encountered, along the way there also arises obstacles which we may not have considered. Some of the obstacles may be relatively insignificant, while others seem impossible to overcome. This is a critical time in your goal plan as these unforeseen obstacles often lead to discouraging feelings and possibly even fear. It is often an emotional crisis of sorts and a critical crossroads which leads to one of two alternative actions: Either you "decide" to abandon the pursuit of the goal or you "choose" to take on the obstacles and continue moving forward towards the goal. Making excuses and laying blame is simply an admission of defeat or an attempt to rationalize to oneself that the goal was not worthy of attaining in the first place. Ultimately, the choice is yours. Irrespective of the choice you make, the process is the same: Each person will return to their comfort zone of inaction while others will move forward to their success. Obtain the goal. Change the knowledge, attitudes, and procedures of the past that led to the goal. Enjoy the increased confidence and motivation that comes with each new success.

Obstacles are the very essence of growth. Our willingness to face them head-on is the key difference between those who succeed in accomplishing their goals and those who allow fateful dreams to be shattered by inaction. When setting goals, it is important to anticipate potential obstacles which may prevent you from achieving your goal. Those who do not take the time to recognize and act on potential shortfalls see their goals as dreams which they reached for and not as logical targets for which they aimed. It is only natural that we feel initial excitement about a new goal which will keep us moving forward in its early stages; however, an increased intrinsic motivation to accomplish the goal emerges as we move forward and suddenly begin to face a new array of challenges. In other words, you create enthusiasm when you take action and action results in increased confidence. This increased confidence is an intrinsic result of the production activity which represents an increased perception of a lack of external motivation. Increased confidence generates a goal that no longer appears to be an esoteric dream, but one that has become a logical target in the early stages of the action.

5.1. Identifying Challenges

Mind mapping is an excellent technique that focuses on all aspects of life; as well as family, work, physical health, and emotional well-being. Mind mapping is an excellent exercise in identifying all of our personal challenges because it concentrates on all aspects of our lives - emotional, physical, mental, social, or career. The mind is divided into six units and each of these units are then expanded with branches. In this way, the individual gains a better understanding of how the units interact with each other. According to the author, when one can "map" areas in life and understand the problems in each sector of life that may need adjustment to achieve a balance and reach our personal goals.

We all have dreams and goals we would like to achieve. Realizing our individual dreams and aspirations is what gives our lives significance. However, the desire to achieve our full potential in life can be thwarted by life's many challenges. Some of these personal challenges we experience because human nature has a tendency to resist negative forces. When we cannot seem to reach our goals, we experience frustration and helplessness; we then blame "fate" for our inability to achieve. When dealing with career, emotional, family, or financial issues, it is important to identify the particular challenges that should be overcome. Identifying these issues must be the first step in order to improve our opportunities to achieve our goals.

5.2. Strategies for Success

People successful in their careers often set broad, long-term goals. They define what success would look like for them in their fields, and then set up a strategic plan that includes the steps they need to perform to accomplish their long-term vision. Often it helps to write these long-term goals including the planned daily actions on a regular basis as a reminder. Similarly, successful people also set long-term goals in other areas of their lives such as learning new skills, acquiring valuable physical assets, taking all planned vacations with family. But for their personal lives, their emphasis is on short-term goals. Their focus is to be healthy, happy and absolutely delighted with their lives every day.

Another common characteristic of many successful individuals is that they are goal-oriented. Success experts from around the world teach that one way to become successful is to set a long-term goal and then work on smaller goals to reach the end. These shorter goals eventually add up to meeting the longer goal. By working toward something that we believe in, we become excited about our life. We have something to look forward to and something to share with others. Goal setting is the first step to attaining success. This can be done in all aspects of our life.

It is possible to increase your chances for success. Strategies for success include setting long- and short-term goals and learning perseverance, self-discipline and hard work. Strategic planning can lead to success. People who have studied successful people say that true success is more than just reaching a high social status or level of affluence. They say the truly successful person is one who masters their ego. They have learned to enjoy the person that they are becoming and find happiness in their own accomplishments and the things that make life interesting and fun.

CHAPTER 6

Staying Motivated

But, doing the same old thing will only lead to the same old effects. However, I can say with conviction that we can hang on and stagnate until it is right. If we utilize or optimize 48 soil methods or procedures if we fail to do so, we may reduce our well-being and well-being. Then, find the appropriate way to find self-improvement and inner peace and strength. When you're done - see everything you've achieved, how you worked without being lazy, how you struggled to earn money, and the guaranteed happiness and prosperity you've achieved. Then - maintain this alignment by staying excited and energetic about your main block of gratitude.

6. Staying motivated. We've all been there - where we should be working hard on revising our book, creating our book proposal to attract a good agent, scanning marketplaces, businesses and web duplications of how we're going to set up our book - but because we think overpowered - powered by our problems, experiences and feelings that reflect on each other every day. If we don't quit our assurance autopilot and take a stab at it all by ourselves, these factors will always lead to the formation of future expressions that will damage us good standing in existence except for their innermost

worlds. Our thoughts may keep us in situations of our top-notch, significant existence, and glib perfection. To help us do this, some professionals may endorse that we set out to follow any new procedure and anyone who has not passed this exam en masse will be suspended until January 2022.

6.1. Finding Inspiration

Being independent. All people want to feel independent. They want to do things for themselves and to stand on their own. To be financially independent is always a goal and therefore a personal inspiration. This can take on the form of setting business or personal goals and then working towards and attaining these goals. Whether we are working towards it, or if we are there, this is also a highly motivating aspect. Everyone wants to be above average. One of the best ways to find inspiration is to find someone who has succeeded in the way that you would like to and then to follow their example. Get to know what they did, how they did it and why they did it and then follow suit. This often becomes a positive feedback cycle as well. Every time you take a step and it works, being in someone else's footsteps inspires you to take another step, which again works and again inspires you and so the cycle continues towards success. The final piece of inspiration comes from evidence of how well what you are doing is working out. Every time you see how well you are doing, or every time you visualize yourself doing even better, this added inspiration will work like mini pushes towards your ultimate goal.

While it is easy to say that you are going to chase your dreams, or that you want financial independence, or that you would like to attain a certain academic standard, finding the inspiration to do these things is much tougher. As much as anybody can ever tell you that you must be financially successful or must be happy with what you've attained in your academic career, the motivation to do so must come from you. Nobody can make you do it if you don't want to. People can push you and give you directions, but if you aren't motivated to succeed, it is useless as you simply won't do the work it takes to achieve that success. There are a number of reasons for finding this inspiration you require and they can include:

6.2. Rewarding Progress

It is human nature to crave rewards. The continued presence or promise of a reward serves to raise dopamine levels in the brain, thereby supplying energy to fulfill the reward expectation. There are also instances when an unexpected reward is experienced as even more pleasurable than the reward which was anticipated. Skinnerian psychology has shown that intermittent reinforcement ideally yields a higher response rate compared to continuous reinforcement. As humans, the unpredictable nature of intermittent reinforcement creates a constant state of excitement and eager anticipation. The successful accomplishment of a goal is synonymous with a reward. Our reward response is doubled in instances where we are told "thank you" by a peer or supervisor. Medicinally speaking, praise promotes the release of dopamine in the brain's reward center. A greater dopamine release promotes higher enthusiasm and personal energy, elevating levels of performance.

Simple rewards are powerful motivators, time and time again. Our society is based upon the premise of gaining rewards and attaining the appraisals of fellow human beings. However, too many people rely solely upon external rewards, failing to recognize the internal satisfaction that can be evoked by the act of self-effort during goal achievement. The energy spent in waiting for an external reward is futile when there is an opportunity to cherish the reward of the present moment instead. This self-appreciated reward serves to reinvigorate and motivate subsequent efforts.

CHAPTER 7

Tracking Progress

The next step coincides with reviewing goals daily. Focused time should be allotted at the conclusion of the day. This is when the project calendar becomes the morning wake-up. Gaps formulated from the calendar travelling beyond the daily tasks are recorded. This self-review sets the stage for the next day determination. You know what works for you, but it is very important to set up a concrete tracking system for your goal. I suggest listing the action steps, in their proper sequence, and posting it somewhere prominent. Then, as you take each step, go back and check it off the list. Again, the act of checking it off reduces the stress and negativity, and increases the momentum and spontaneity, associated with the act of actually doing important stuff!

It does little good to set a goal, only to stop thinking about it. Memory fades with time. Rarely is the initial enthusiasm of setting a goal enough to maintain motivation through completion. Writing down each step, tracking progress and reviewing the goals daily helps to reinforce the original intention. The purpose of writing down the goal is to pause and reflect what has been done in the previous steps. The critical benefit occurs when the 'so what' question becomes the action steps. For each item, there may be several steps to consider. A project calendar can be addressed. Factors such as time will give indication of whether completion will need adjustment. This calendar is to monitor process, not overpower the steps of functionality. After 30 days, a review should occur with the assistance of the project calendar.

7.1. Monitoring Goals

7.1.1 Results Monitoring: Performance indicates whether or not the product is achieved. It shows the real and full view where one stands. Measures can be quantified for performance which leads to enhancement and efficiencies in individual's productivity. It can also explicitly define desired goals. It pelts all aspects of a person's units and competencies. The main components which have to be monitored during the setting of the goals are: % Quantity % quality % cost % Timeliness Gain through improvement in accessing using up to the level of individual's performance.

Monitoring is an ongoing effort, but it is also a time to reflect, adjust and focus. To keep them on track, both progress and problems areas should be reviewed. Monitoring of measures helps to reach up to the goals when achieved. When goals are not achieved and the target are not reached they not only help to keep us thoughtful and reflect on what really has an eye on of learning from while also revisiting previous parts and focusing on missed parts. Process Monitoring helps to capture the activities and the approaches used and to ensure that residual issues are resolved in a timely manner. The implementation plan should include methods to monitor the approaches to achieve the objectives adapted in agency strategic plans. Performance measures and goals should be regularly collected, analyzed, and distributed to review progress towards the completion of performance goals in the final account.

The setting of the goal does not stop here. An essential part of the recuperation of the setting of a goal is the capacity to have the ability to monitor the approaches.

7.2. Adjusting Strategies

Are you motivated enough that you will keep pushing yourself to achieve your goal once things become difficult? Will push through when you'd rather do something else? Another way to check if your goal is within reach is whether or not you are making progress. Ask yourself these questions: Am I currently moving toward my goal, even if the progress is slow? Can I realistically and effectively see myself doing what it will take to achieve my goal in the future? They work in all areas and are especially feared in situations we may not be as familiar with – talking with people we are interested in talking to.

If you aren't reaching your goals, or are having problems achieving them, the problem may not be the goal, but the strategy you are using. If you are doing things that aren't moving you toward success, you need to change what you are doing. Sometimes this doesn't work, though, because the best or only strategy for achieving a goal won't work, so you need a different goal. First, make sure your goal is something you really want to do. Will you enjoy it? Will it make you happy? Will you find fulfillment or satisfaction in it? Just imagine your life after you have achieved your goal, will you be fulfilled and satisfied?

CHAPTER 8

Celebrating Achievements

Good feelings are linked to celebration. Celebrating accomplishments leads not only to an improved outlook on life, but also to greater optimism, increased coping abilities, improved physical health, and a heightened sense of psychological well-being. These feelings can reverse the effects of negative emotions, such as fear, worthlessness, despair, and anxiety, that typically limit our focus, limits the processing of information, and limits our creativity. When emotions are turned around by celebration, our focus can be restored, attention increases, creative thinking improves, and we are able to look for opportunity and success. Celebrating while personalized reward mechanisms are powerful and similar strategies can rapidly be applied.

Celebrating achievements acknowledges milestones in the journey towards the completion of the final big-picture goal, provides motivation and illustrates the realization of the end goal. By acknowledging what we have accomplished, we realize more fully what we are capable of doing. This belief in ourselves drives our motivation higher and pushes us towards achieving our next milestone. While rewards themselves can be very powerful motivators, the simple act of celebration can also provide motivation. Celebration shows that we have accomplished a particular task - the first of several milestones - and demonstrates that we are capable of recognizing our achievement and acting to reward ourselves accordingly. Achievements play an important role in the goal setting process, providing opportunities for achievement, and are linked with goal progress and motivation.

8.1. Recognizing Success

Being happy doesn't mean it is one great big explosive moment and from now on, life is just perfect. We all know it isn't. Life has its ups and downs. Being happy means drawing joy from the small things as much as the grand things. It is the series of baby steps you may or may not even see, that enable you to work your way towards the goal and the daily recognitions of those baby steps. It's your children hugging and saying, "I love you," a phone call or text from a friend, a moment of solitude, even cleaning a room. These things don't necessarily make it an "explosive" day, but they do make it a good day! That's not to say that there won't be bad days. But we just handle it with stride and shift our focus onto recognizing the good moments. Because the good moments are what really matter when we strive to be the happy, joyful, successful person we all want to be!

One of the main reasons people fail to achieve their goals is due to unrealistic expectations. They believe the achievement of the goal will be grand, thrilling, and stupendous. But often, when the time comes, the feeling is actually letdown, disappointment, and a little glum. Why? Because they were expecting fireworks, and they got one sparkler. The failure to achieve the sparkler might have been because the sparkler failed to materialize, or it was a day of full-blown fireworks that terrify the dog, or it was just a day of everyday living experiences. And then the person comes away saying, "Why did I bother? This isn't anything great." Recognizing success is all about celebrating the small achievements. Because recognizing the small steps towards reaching the ultimate goal is really what keeps us moving forward.